CW00673041

TEN DARTMOOR TORS

John Earle

First published in Great Britain in 2009, reprinted 2012

British Library Cataloguing-in-Publication Data
A CIP record for this title is available from the British Library

ISBN 978 1 906887 07 0

PiXZ Books
Halsgrove House, Ryelands Business Park,
Bagley Road, Wellington, Somerset TA21 9PZ
Tel: 01823 653777
Fax: 01823 216796
email: sales@halsgrove.com

An imprint of Halstar Ltd, part of the Halsgrove group of companies
Information on all Halsgrove titles is available at: www.halsgrove.com

Printed and bound in China by Toppan Leefung Printing Ltd

Contents

How to use this book

I hope this book will take you on some great adventures to climb ten tors on Dartmoor and have a look at some of the extraordinary and interesting things near them. The word tor, by the way, comes from the Celtic "Twr" meaning a tower.

Dartmoor is the largest wilderness area in southern England and has great beauty as well as being a wild, lonely and remote upland. When you are out on the moor there are always the rolling, sweeping horizons and huge skies all around you and a strange indefinable scent that changes with the seasons. Sometimes the misty air is full of smell of the damp, peaty moorland, at other times the pungent smell of gorse or the sweet honey-scent of purple heather. Listen and you will hear the tinkling sound of countless streams and rivers tumbling off the moor to the sea, while high overhead the skylarks pour out their own evocative, liquid song and the solitary buzzard wheels overhead mewing like a kitten.

You will not be making first ascents of the tors I shall be telling you about. Probably Bronze Age man did that about 4000 years ago! Nor will it be like the Golden Age of mountaineering in the Alps at the end of the19th century when those peaks were climbed for the first time. But I am sure you will have a sense of achievement and excitement if you get round all ten tors and you will indeed be climbing the Everest of Dartmoor, Yes Tor.

A word of warning. Dartmoor is a high, dangerous upland area where the weather can change in moments and, of course, you will have heard about the thick mists and the quaking bogs; need I mention the Hound of the Baskervilles?! But what I am saying is you must wear the right clothes and boots. You need to take warm sweaters or fleeces, a hat and gloves and really good waterproofs, even in summer. A small rucksack is useful to carry your spare clothing, food for the day, a water bottle or Thermos, and a small first aid kit.

While there are sketch maps in this book you do need to be able to read and use a map and compass. The best one, but it is quite large and awkward to use on a windy, wet day, is the Outdoor Leisure 28 Series also known as the Explorer Series for Dartmoor. The scale is 1:25 000, 4cm to 1km or 2.5 inches to 1 mile. Or there is the Landranger Series with a scale of 1:50 000, 2cm to 1km or 1.25 inches to 1 mile. You will need Sheets 191 and 202 to cover both north and south Dartmoor.

Most of the walks are circular but it is quite possible to shorten some of them by cutting off corners or even starting at a different place to the one I suggest.

I am not giving the time each walk takes as everyone walks at a different pace and, also, I hope that you will not want to rush around as fast as you can, but take some time to soak up the views, atmosphere and grandeur of Dartmoor and look closely at the extraordinary things that I have written about, not to mention having a brief stop at some of the pubs, inns and cafés near the walks.

If you would like read more details about some of the incredible sites you will be visiting then you will find them in my book *Dartmoor: Walks into History* also published by Halsgrove.

Good walking, and I hope you enjoy your ten tors. At least you wont have altitude problems on Dartmoor like you would in the Alps or Himalayas but I must say I get pretty puffed on some of the steep hills these days!

Useful telephone numbers

Dartmoor National Park Authority. 01626 832093
The Dartmoor Trust which runs the *Dartmoor Archive* (pictures of Dartmoor on line) website at www.dartmoorarchive.org" Office. 01752 837265
High Moorland Visitor Centre, Princetown. 01822 890414
Weather Forecasts. 0891 500404.
Firing on Dartmoor Ranges. Freephone. 0800 458 4868.

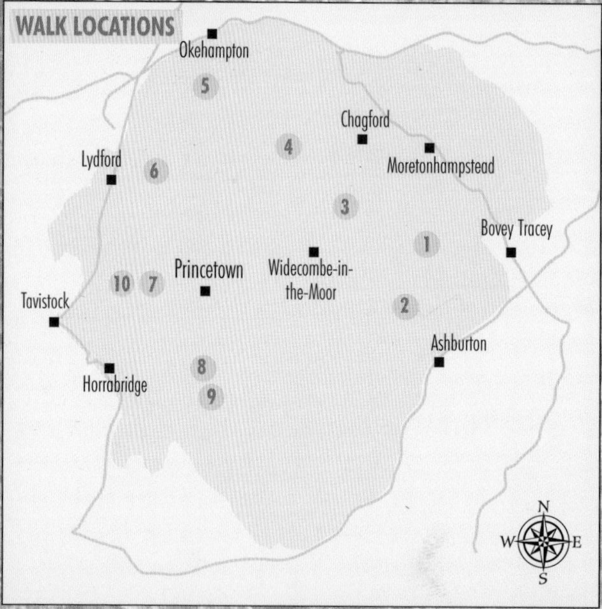

Key to Symbols Used

WALK LOCATIONS

Okehampton
5
Chagford
4
Moretonhampstead
Lydford
6
3
Bovey Tracey
1
Princetown
Widecombe-in-the-Moor
10 7
Tavistock
2
Ashburton
8
Horrabridge
9
N
W E
S

Map symbols:

Park & start

Tarred Road

Footpath

Building

Pub

Level of difficulty:

Easy

Fair

More challenging 

1 Hay Tor

Climb the most iconic tor of Dartmoor, have a look at a granite railway and the industry of times past.

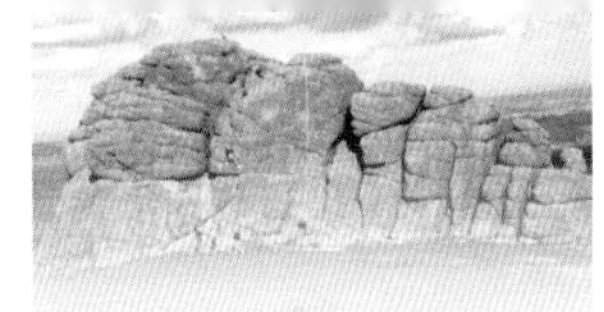

I suppose that Hay Tor is the most iconic of all the Dartmoor Tors and the one most visited when people come to the moors. You can see it for miles around, from the South Hams, Torquay, and even coming down Haldon Hill from Exeter on the A38. It is therefore quite right that this should be the first tor to climb. The only trouble is that, during the holiday periods, you may one of hundreds trying to get to the top. And while it is fun to climb up the cut steps in the granite to get the marvellous panoramic views, there are many other interesting things to see nearby, away from the crowds. I have given three starting car parks but I think that the first one below Saddle Tor is the best as it is far less crowded.

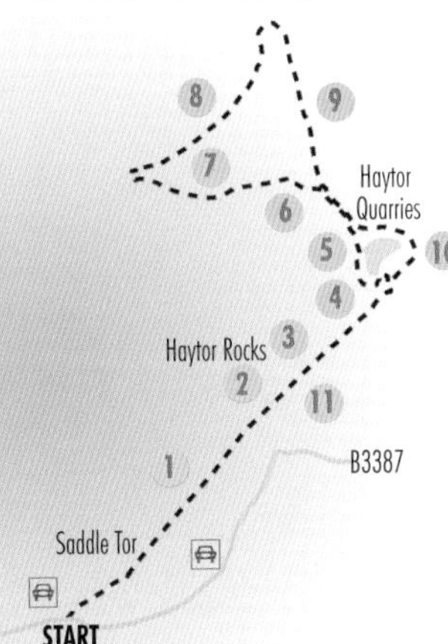

Level: 🥾🥾
Length: 4.5 miles
Terrain: Fairly level moorland with a few sheep tracks to follow through bracken, heather and gorse.
Park & Start ref: SX 748762 or SX 758767 or SX 765772.

However you may want to start from one of the other two, or just call in either to get an ice cream from one of the vans parked there, or at the lower car park to visit and have a look around the Dartmoor National Park's new Visitor Centre, where there is also a loo by the way.

1 From the car park at Saddle Tor set off up the path north-east that leads to the col (gap) between the two summits. From here you will see the huge rock face of Low Man across a stretch of moorland about three-quarters of a mile away. When you reach it you will appreciate its size for it is the largest natural rock face actually on Dartmoor. There are some excellent and extremely severe rock climbs on it, some of which are over 150 feet, but one of the less hair-raising ones is called Raven's Gully which goes up the obvious cleft on the left of the face as you look at it. You may well see climbers here.

2 Walk and scramble round to the left below Low Man until you are in the wide grassy bay with Hay Tor on the other side. If you would like to climb Low Man (another summit for you!) walk along round the rock until you see some steps cut into the granite with an iron handrail and rungs on the south east side of the tor overlooking the upper car park.

3 Come back down and now walk across to Hay Tor itself. There are many good rock climbs here too, but if you wish to get easily to the top there is a flight of steps cut into

Looking across to Greator Rocks, Hound Tor and Cosdon Beacon from Holwell quarries.

Standing as they do on the south-eastern edge of Dartmoor, the views from both these tors are magnificent. To the south, the coast with Torbay and Lyme Bay are visible. To the north-west the moors stretches as far as you can see to Cawsands Beacon or Cosdon Hill. East you can make out Lawrence Castle or Haldon Belvedere near Exeter.

the granite here too, so go around to the east side. These steps caused considerable indignant wrath of a certain Dr Crocker who denounced them as far back as 1851 as 'the unsightly stair step'. I wonder what he would have thought of the hundreds that climb to the top today, including you of course!

4 From the far side of Hay Tor take the path that runs down the hill to the north-east to some granite spoil tips and a wire fence. Follow the fence round until you come to a gate that leads into the quarry with its lakes.

5 Go around to the west (Hay Tor) side of the largest pond and follow the stony path north along the edge of the water for about 75 yards until you come to a stile in a gully. Climb over this and follow the track in the gully out onto the open moor.

After a while the path has a left fork which you take, until you soon reach some points in the granite railway at a cross roads of the tracks.

Hay Tor quarries.

These are the remarkable granite rails of the tramway on which huge, flat trucks ran, pulled by as many as 19 horses which transported the granite all the way down to Teigngrace and the Teign estuary to be taken by ship to London. Here you can see the points and the flanges cut in the granite rails where the wooden wheels of the trucks ran.

7 Cross over the main line and take the path down the hill following the rails. You will see ahead

of you a jumble of waste mounds and tips below Holwell Tor and you will soon be at Holwell Quarries.

8 Retrace your steps back past the quarry and there is a decision to make about the route. After a while, as you begin to start the climb back, you will see a small path branching off left through the deep bracken in summer and contouring round the slope to Smallacombe Rocks. If you would like a good view across to Greator Rocks, some lakes in the valley and Hound Tor, and maybe have a look for the Bronze Age hut circles, then follow that track. If not then plod on up the track you came down until you reach the granite rails at the top.

Quarrymen's Hut, Holwell quarries.

9 If you went to Smallcombe Rocks there is a good grassy track that runs south-east back to the granite rails and the path you came down from the Hay Tor Quarries. If you retraced your steps up hill to the rails both routes are now back together. Follow the track you came down originally from the quarries until you see a minor path cutting off left towards the huge spoil tips and ramps.

10 Walk round the end of the tips until you get to some rather scruffy pine trees.

The Rock Inn Haytor Vale.

This flat area is where there were huts and small houses where the quarrymen lived, both here and also in houses down in Haytor Vale, where there is an excellent pub, by the way, called The Rock Inn

11 I am afraid that there is no other way back to your car than to walk up to Hay Tor and Low Man and across to Saddle Tor but you might want to drop down to the Dartmoor National Park Information Centre at the lower car park or to have an Ice Cream at either of the car parks before the journey back.

Hay Tor and Low Man from Hound Tor.

The Granite Railway, Hay Tor.

2 Rippon Tor

A long climb up to a summit on the edge of Dartmoor to view some strange carvings, Bronze Age cairns, and down to where an old pub stood, and the remains of a medieval longhouse.

Level:
Length: 3.5 miles
Terrain: A long climb at the start but most of the walk is on tracks across moorland.
Park & Start ref: SX739747.

The start is near Cold East Cross which is a splendidly apt name. It is a bitter place. Whenever there is mist, rain, frost or snow on Dartmoor you will find it here; probably all four! About 400 yards north of the crossroads, along the road, you will see a lay-by and a track on your left where you can park. Widecombe-in-the-Moor is nearby with two pubs.

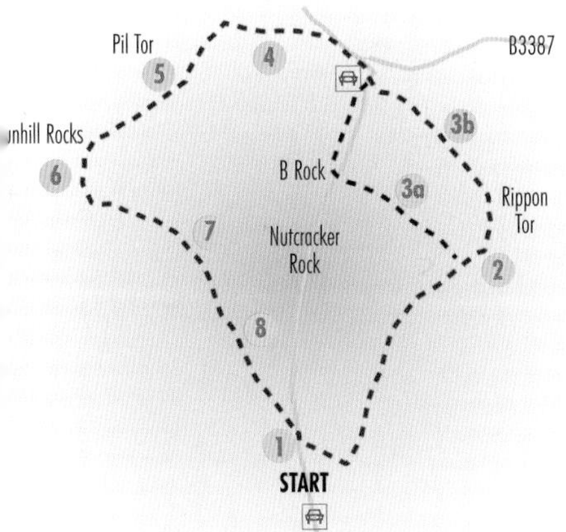

The Rugglestone Inn Widecombe-in-the-Moor.

1 Walk back about 100 yards south, parallel to the road, until you reach a gate set back in a recess on the opposite side. Cross over and go through making sure you shut the gate after you. You can now take the fairly rough track that climbs up the hill immediately to your left, if you want to have a close look at the Nutcracker Rock. If not, walk on towards another gate ahead of you and go through that before climbing up left on an easier path up the hill beside the wall and fence. If we went up the left hand track you can wander across to look at the Nutcracker Rock but you can easily see it from the other path as well.

As you walk you will see, away to your right, a large, squat, brick construction further east and down the hill. These are the butts of what was once the Rippon Tor Rifle Range that closed in the 1970s.

2 At the top of both routes you will come to a gate in the wall. Go through and now aim up the path towards the summit of Rippon Tor.

View from the summit of Rippon Tor looking towards Saddle Tor, Low Man and Hay Tor.

There are many things to see on the summit of Rippon Tor at 1560 feet. There are amazing views over the south coast and inland over Dartmoor.
The huge mounds of rock on your right are Bronze Age burial cairns.
About 30 yards north-west of the summit down the hill you will find a curious, unfinished stone cross cut in relief in the living rock.
30 yards further down the hill by some rocks there is an unfinished mill-stone or cheese press, and two more unfinished carved stones nearby.

3 There is a choice of routes now. (a) You can follow the path north-west down to the road junction at Hemsworthy Gate and walk back south beside the road to the B Rock and the remains of Newhouse, but then back again to the junction to go up Top Tor. (b) Walk back down the way you came to the gate in the wall and then follow, on the Rippon Tor side of the wall, north-west down to the road and B Rock. Go through the gate into the road. You will see lying beside the road a flat rock with 'A' carved on it and the date 1793. This is the boundary stone for the parish of Ashburton. Further along the road there are a few standing stones, low walls and a grassy yard. These are the remains of Newhouse, a travellers and carters pub, burnt down many years ago.

Unfinished cross carved from the living rock below the summit of Rippon Tor.

Ashburton boundary stone.

The last landlord was called Foale and on the map you will see Foale's Arrishes; Arrish is Devonian for field.

4 If you followed route (b) walk parallel to the road north to the road junction at Hemsworthy Gate. Next swing more or less west up the path to Top Tor with Foale's Arrishes on your left where there are also some Bronze Age and Iron Age settlements and fields systems.

Dartmoor longhouses date from the medieval period and were a more conventional house shape, with a central door and cross passage. The family lived at the 'uphill' end of the house and the animals lived in the other end.

From Top Tor walk across to Pil Tor and then there is a good path that leads down to Tunhill Rocks where there are Bronze Age hut circles and really good views over the Widecombe-in-the-Moor valley.

Remains of the Newhouse Inn below Foale's Arrishes.

6 Quite a small path runs south now which you follow until you reach an obvious made up track.

7 Follow the track south-east until you are about 200 yards from the ford and you will see hidden in the bracken, in summer, the remains of an old, medieval longhouse just below the track to your left.

8 Walk back up to the track and then keep on down to Blackslade Ford and climb up the hill to the road and your car.

3 Hookney Tor

Fine views across the moors, the remains of tin mines, a look at what was an old pub, amazing Bronze Age remains, and burial mounds or cairns of prehistoric date.

The start is at Bennett's Cross where there is a car park nearby.
The Warren House Inn is only half a mile away.

If you wanted just to look at Grimspound then there is a lay-by SX697809

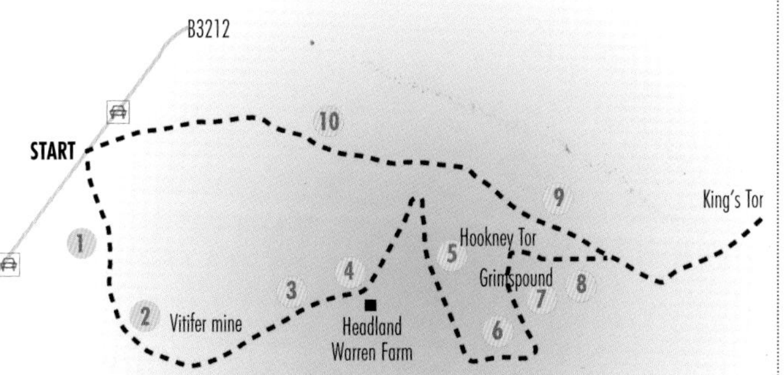

Level: ♥♥♥
Length: 5.5 miles
Terrain: Several steep climbs but mainly on tracks across moorland.
Park & Start ref: SX681817

Bennett's Cross is also a boundary marker. W.B. cut into the stone is for Warren Bounds. The cross is said to be named after William Benet who was a juror in the Tinner's Parliament in the reign of Henry VIII.

Hut circles in Grimspound.

1 Set off south following the small path through the heather. Don't take the path that runs east marked on the map as The Two Moors Way; you'll be coming back that way.

You will see off to your left deep gullies called gerts which were dug by the tin miners from the Birch Tor and Vitifer Mines.

2 The path reaches the bottom of the valley and goes close to an old wheel pit on your right and a stream and then, in a lovely, grassy, flat area, there are the ruins of some old mine buildings.

Mining was still carried out here until the 1930s. The mines here were over 77 fathoms deep and there would have been leats, water wheels for pumps, crushing mills, a miner's dry, barracks, a count house and many other buildings. If you have a mind to you can go on down the valley to the Golden Dagger Mine but you'd have to walk back

3 You will see a track leading up the hill towards the east which you follow. Once again you will be close to some deep gerts. When you reach the col (gap) you could climb in and out of the gullies to the south to have a look at a triple Bronze Age stone row. Look at the map.

4 Walk on down the track now towards Headland Warren Farm.

5 Follow the path that climbs up to the road where you turn right and walk down to Firth Bridge.

Triple stone row on Headland Warren.

Grimspound is one of the most famous antiquities on Dartmoor. It is a Bronze Age pound and village over 4000 years old, where they kept their animals safe behind a high double wall over 500 yards in circumference and lived in small round huts built of granite with thatched roofs.

6 Leave the road and follow the obvious path east up to Grimspound.

7 Follow the well made stone path north steeply upwards to Hookney Tor, your summit at 1640 feet, with marvellous views over the moors.

Grimspound from Hookney Tor.

8 Just to the north-east of Hookney Tor, about 30 feet away, there is a small subsidiary tor with an indistinct sheep's track leading to it. Take that and then look across to the north-east to see King's Barrow, a low bump on the skyline about a kilometre away. Aim at that across very rough ground with tussocks and heather until you reach a grassy track. There are a few sheep tracks to follow. Turn right along the track and follow this until you see a small path cutting off left through the heather towards King's Barrow with quite a number of old weather-beaten poles along it. Follow this past the poles up to King's Barrow. You could cheat if you wished to and not go as far as King's Barrow. In which case

The strange wooden posts here and also found on Hamel Down were put here by the Home Guard during the Second World War to stop German parachutists and gliders landing: 'They don't like it up 'em, you know!'

The huge pile of stones of King's Barrow, with a dip in the middle, might be the burial place of one of the chieftains from Grimspound though there is no proof of this. Sadly it has been badly disturbed by treasure seekers and some of the stones have been robbed for building.

from Hookney Tor take a broad, easy, grassy path almost north which will take you to a gap in the ruined wall by the standing stones. (See 9.)

9 Retrace your steps back down the path to the larger track and then turn right and follow it running north-west and along the wall. Go through a gap in the ruined wall with some fine standing stones and you will you see the path cutting downhill left to the west, marked on the map as The Two Moors Way.

10 Cross the road and take the well trodden Two Moors Way that goes up the hill with Birch Tor on your left and then finally down the hill towards Bennett's Cross and the end of the walk.

Headland Warren Farm.

4 Kestor Rock

Climb another tor and walk to ancient Bronze Age stone rows and a stone circle: look at a rock with a hole in it and see two clapper bridges.

Park in the lay-by near the entrance to Batworthy House.

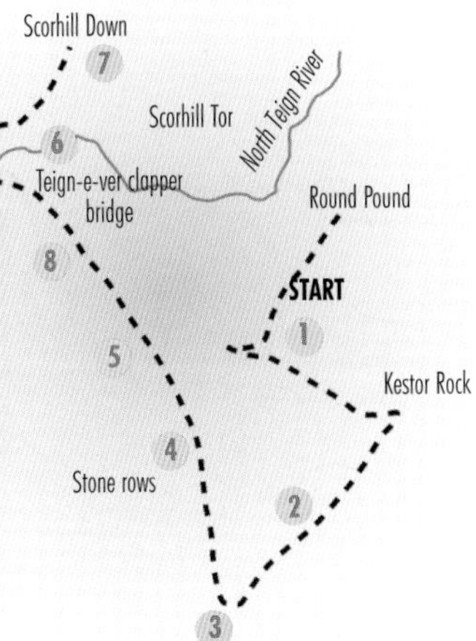

The Longstone is a very old boundary marker of the Forest of Dartmoor, first mentioned in 1240, but was probably put up by the Bronze Age people many thousands of years before. It is 10.5 feet high and has 'C' for Chagford and 'G' for Gidleigh parish boundaries and 'DC' for the Duchy of Cornwall carved on it.

Level:
Length: 3.75 miles
Terrain: Fairly easy walking over open moorland.
Park & Start ref: SX663865.

The Longstone with Kestor rock behind.

1 Walk back a little down the road (you could go and have a look at Round Pound if you wished) and then strike uphill to Kestor Rock on the skyline; slightly awkward going with many tussocks but there are a few sheep tracks. Seen for miles around along the eastern edge of the moor the Kestor is a fine viewpoint. There are deep eroded rock basins on the summit and holes where the uprights of iron railings once stood.

2 Strike out now south-west aiming at a tall standing stone called the Longstone just over half a mile away.

3 Walk on south for just over 200 yards and you will see a

Round Pond an Iron Age settlement.

As you drove here you may have seen on your right, about 300 yards back from your start point, a large stone circle. This is Round Pound and dates from the Iron Age and is only one of two such settlements on Dartmoor, most of them being Bronze Age.

single block of granite called the Three Boys.

The Three Boys was once the cover stone of a dolmen (burial chamber), or Kistvaen (stone coffin,) and there were probably three stones creating the grave site, hence the name.

4 You must go back to the Longstone now and continue north past an amazing collection of double stone rows and standing stones. If you look around you will see that there is an unusual multiple stone circle, the largest is about 29 feet across but it encloses three others. Lying nearby there are two fallen menhirs. When standing they must have made an impressive entrance to the circle with the stone rows leading away back to the Three Boys where perhaps a tribal leader was buried.

5 Set off north to Batworthy Corner by the wall and then follow it along for just under three-

Teign-e-ver Clapper Bridge.

The Tolmen, or Holed Stone.

quarters of a mile down to North Teign River and the oddly named Teign-e-ver Bridge, one of two clapper bridges here, the other spanning the Walla Brook.

6 It might interest you to follow the main River Teign downstream for about 50 yards to look at the extraordinary Tolmen or Holed Stone.

Scorhill stone circle.

7 Walk back to the bridge and then follow the track up hill over the Gidleigh Leat by another clapper bridge until you reach Scorhill Circle.

8 Nothing for it I am afraid but to walk back the way you came over the bridges and follow the wall back to Batworthy Corner and round to your car. I always think however that the views walking back over a route are so different it really is worth the journey.

Scorhill is an unusual multiple stone circle, the largest is about 29 feet across but it encloses three others. Lying nearby are two fallen menhirs.

Yes Tor and Mill Tor.

5 Yes Tor and High Willhays

Climb the highest peaks of Dartmoor at 2032 and 2038 feet and enjoy the views across to Exmoor.

You must check to see if there is firing on the Okehampton Ranges before you start this walk. You will have driven past Fice's Cross and Okehampton Camp and through Moor Gate after which you turn right and drive south-west along the wall beside Moor Brook. You can park anywhere along here near Anthony Stile.

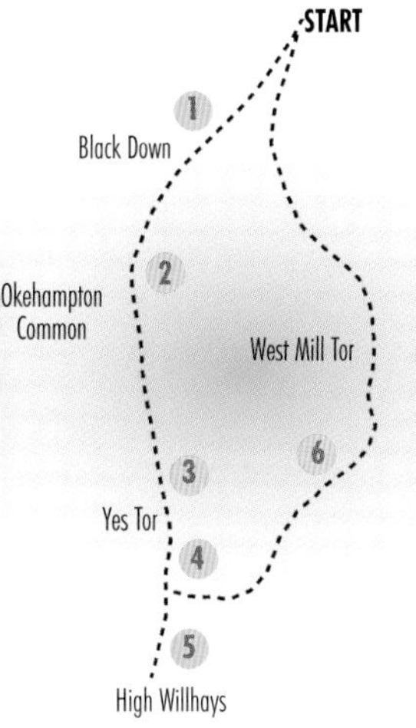

Level:
Length: 6.25 miles
Terrain: Some tracks but also rough, rocky moorland.
Park & Start ref: SX588926.
Public transport: Nearest in Okehampton
Refreshments: There are many good pubs and cafés in Okehampton

The use of the National Park of Dartmoor by the military is a controversial subject but they have been here since the early 1800s. Okehampton Camp was built in 1895. The moor's use went up again during the Boer War 1899 and the Great War. During World War II the whole of Dartmoor was used for training and it remains a major training area to this day. Red flags warn of firing ranges in use. For times when access is prohibited phone 0800 458 4868.

Yes Tor and Mill Tor, with Moor Brook.

1 From here roads and tracks branch off in all directions but to make the climb more adventurous, with a direct ascent, don't follow the metalled track that goes to the east of Mill Tor but take the right fork of the unsurfaced track that climbs up Black Down.

2 At the top another rough track cuts off left and climbs to the gap between Mill Tor and Yes Tor which you can take to avoid the rough direct ascent (See 3). Or a little further along you will see a wide, low ramp that runs south almost directly towards Yes Tor past a pond in wet weather. You could follow that and drop down to Red-a-ven Brook. Or finally you could keep on along the track that also swings south to Red-a-ven Brook Ford.

Red-a-ven Brook has the distinction of having its source higher than any other on Dartmoor, at 1800 feet, and indeed many of the rivers of the Pennines. That ramp that you might have followed has occasional sleepers and metal clamps that you will have seen and are all part of an old tramway that carried moving targets for the military to shoot at.

3 It is now a straight, steep climb directly towards your 'Everest', over fairly awkward ground with heather and rocks, but I thought you would relish the challenge! If it is too rough for you then continue up the stream over the moor for just under a mile until you reach a track that climbs south-west and then west up to the broad ridge between Yes Tor and High Willhays. Turn right (north) on the ridge to get to the summit.

Whichever way you got here you will now be on Yes Tor.

Pice's Cross.

Yes Tor was thought, for many years, to be the highest peak of Dartmoor, and it is truly a peak as it is over 2000 feet at 2032 feet. But High Willhays was found to be 2038 feet by the Ordnance Survey so poor old Yes Tor was demoted. Both these peaks are the highest points not only of Dartmoor but the whole of England as far north as Ingleborough in West Yorkshire which is 2363 feet. To the north from here you can look away over a patchwork quilt of fields, woods, farms and river valleys of North Devon and across to north-east Cornwall. On fine days you can see as far as Exmoor and beyond to the Bristol Channel.

The low ramp for the rails of the moving targets once used by the military.

5 Walk south now along the broad summit ridge, a sort of plateau, to the rocks of High Willhays. The views here are not so spectacular and there is not a feeling that you are on a mountain as there is on Yes Tor; but looking south into the depths of Dartmoor are some of the best views that you will find on the moor.

6 Go back north now to the col (gap) and then strike off east down the track which you can now follow all the way back to the start. But if you want to bag another peak then strike up to the summit of West Mill Tor the small, poor relation, with Yes Tor towering above. Then from here go west until the find yet another track that will also take you back to the start via Black Down.

Road leading off into the moor below Yes Tor.

Ford, stepping stones and bridge over the River Lyd.

6 Brat Tor

A poignant memorial, an artist's cross, a bleak house, a failed enterprise and a disused railway.

Follow the lane by the excellent Dartmoor Inn and through the gate which will take you to the car park.

The Dartmoor Inn.

Level:
Length: 6 miles
Terrain: Mostly track but some open moorland.
Park & Start ref: SX526 853
Refreshments: Dartmoor Inn

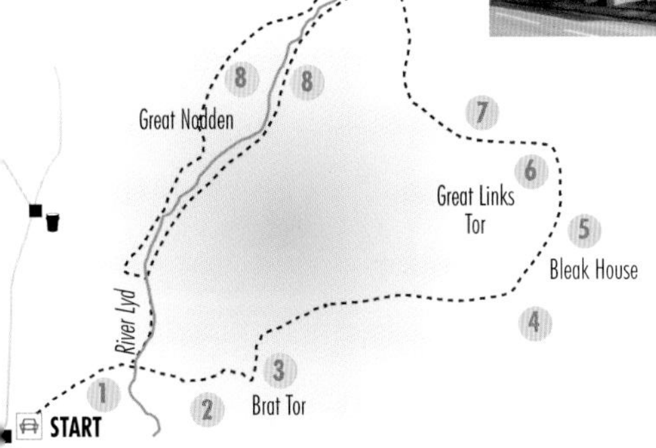

Remains of Rattlebrook Peat Works.

1 Set off along the track by the fence and the downhill to the River Lyd. Don't cross over yet but walk downstream to your right for about 200 yards to a sad reminder of the First World War.

There is a seat and a plaque attached to the rock which reads 'In loving memory of Captain Nigel Duncan Ratcliffe Hunter MC and Bar, Royal Engineers, who was killed in action near Bapaume, on March 25th 1918 aged 23 years.' Nigel clearly loved Dartmoor and here there is a short, poignant poem written by him.

Memorial plaque for Captain Hunter MC.

Walk back now to the bridge or use the stepping stones to cross the river.

2 You will see Widgery Cross standing on the summit of Brat Tor and a steep path leading up to it.

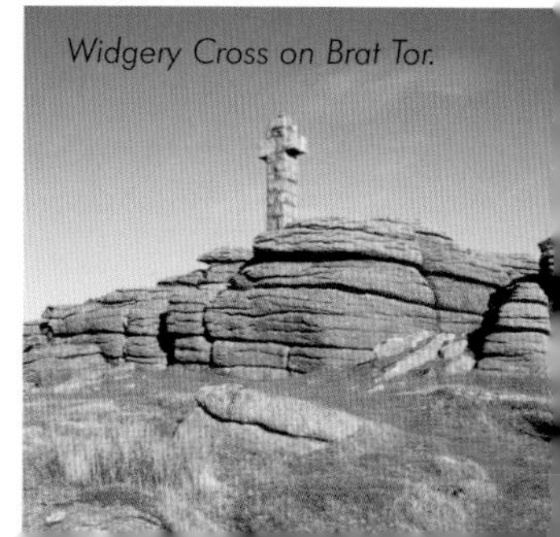

Widgery Cross on Brat Tor.

Widgery cross is made of small blocks of granite rather than from one piece. It was put up at the instigation of the Dartmoor artist William Widgery in 1887 to celebrate the golden jubilee of Queen Victoria. Widgery painted over 3000 pictures in his lifetime. His Dartmoor pictures are still much sought after. The views from here are breathtaking looking across north Devon and down to Cornwall.

The track leading up to Rattlebrook.

3 From the summit of Brat Tor aim north-north-east across the moor until you reach the miner's track. If you wanted to avoid climbing up to Widgery Cross you could have followed this track up from the bridge over the River Lyd.

4 Soon you will begin to swing north into the valley of the Rattle Brook. On your left are the two small tors on the flanks of Great Links Tor called Higher Dunna Goat and Lower Dunna Goat.

5 Keep walking on until you come to the ruins of 'Bleak House' on the far side of the Rattle Brook.

6 Walk on further north and you will come to the remains of the extensive Rattlebrook Peat Works.

The history of cutting peat on Dartmoor for fuel goes back to before Henry III. By 1844 various enterprises had been started here using peat to produce naphtha and moth balls as well as for fuel. Through the rest of the 19th century and into the 20th all kinds of ventures were started and failed here at Rattlebrook but it wasn't until 1955 that the works were finally closed down.

The railway line climbed to over 1000 feet in huge zig-zags. It was built in order to take the peat down to the main line of the old London & South Western Railway.

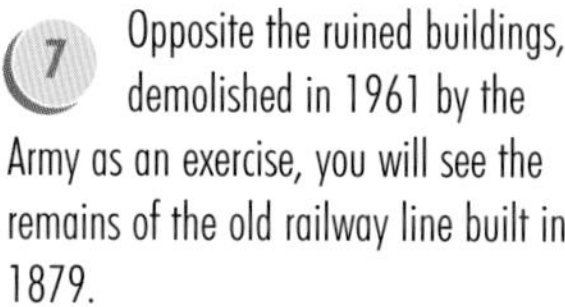

7 Opposite the ruined buildings, demolished in 1961 by the Army as an exercise, you will see the remains of the old railway line built in 1879.

8 You can now follow the old railway track back down to the start past Great Nodden or if you prefer a more direct route you can follow the infant River Lyd back down to your car, from where it flows under the track. Keep an eye out for a tinners' cache, just like a little cave, quite close to the river after you have left the railway track. This route will take you through amazing tinners' works.

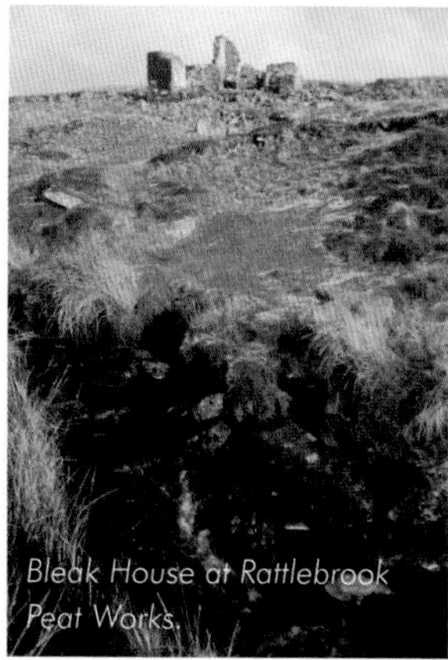

Bleak House at Rattlebrook Peat Works.

A cold day near Higher Dunna Goat.

Ruins of the old school at the start of the King's Tor walk.

7 King's Tor

Remarkable antiquities, a disused railway track and another Dartmoor quarry.

The car park here is the site of what was the highest school in England, built at the start of the First World War, and with a fascinating history.

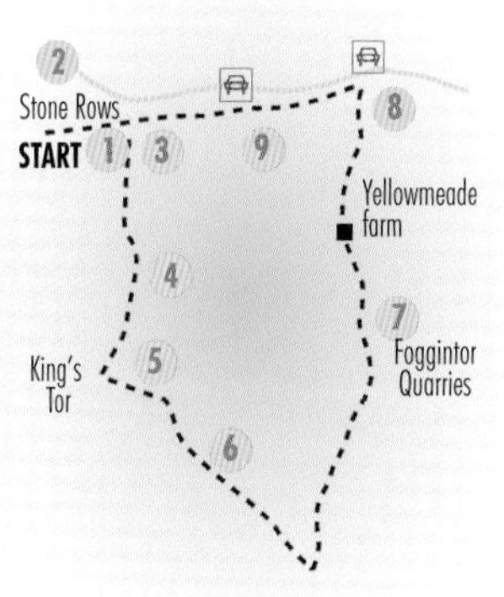

It was for the children of the area but especially for the children of the quarry workers at Foggintor Quarries where you will be going later. It was a fine large building with central heating and floors of wooden parquet blocks. It was closed in 1936 and the headmaster's house became a private residence called 'Four Winds'. Eventually everything became derelict and the school and the house were demolished in the mid 1960s.

Level:
Length: 3 miles
Terrain: Open moorland and tracks.
Park & Start ref: SX561749
Public transport: There are buses across the moor in summer.
Refreshments: Dartmoor Inn at Merrivale

The Dartmoor Inn at Merrivale.

1 Set off west and after about half a mile you will come to one of the most visited and extraordinary stones rows and prehistoric remains on Dartmoor.

The double row of stones is 865 feet long with a large triangular stone blocking the eastern end and a pillar and a slab at the western end. About half way down the avenue is a small stone circle with a ruined barrow in the middle. About 45 feet south of the row is a magnificent kistvaen (grave). The huge covering slab is in two parts as a stonemason cut it in half for a gatepost in 1860.

The double stone row of the Merrivale Antiquities.

King's Tor.

2 You will want to wander about in this amazing area I am sure and there are many things to see.

3 Begin to walk back east now and you will see the remains of an old 17th century track and another standing stone which acted as a marker with 'T' on one side for Tavistock and 'A' for Ashburton carved on the other.

4 Swing south now and drop down to the bottom of the valley to the old tin works. Cross the little stream as best you can and then follow the wall. You will be aiming at King's Tor on the skyline ahead of you. As you begin the climb you will cross the remains of an old railway track.

This line started life in 1823 as the Plymouth and Dartmoor Railway that used horse-drawn trucks, just like the ones at Haytor Quarries, to take granite from the quarries here down to Plymouth. In 1883 it was taken over by the Great Western Railway for passengers and ran all the way up to Princetown. Can you imagine the sight of steam trains running across the moor here? Sadly it was closed in 1965. What a tourist attraction it would make now!

5 If you wanted to you could avoid the climb on up to the summit but just follow the old railway track south-east, but I am sure you will relish the view.

From the summit of King's Tor aim south-east back

Foggintor Quarry is another fascinating place. It is an astonishing area of rock walls and deep lakes. Man wreaked such havoc and destruction and yet when he stopped nature took over and it has all reverted into something beautiful, even magical. It is astonishing to think that over 600 people once lived and worked here. The ruins of this remote community are still to be seen.

Foggintor Quarry.

down to the railway track and follow it until a branch swings north which you take until you are in Foggintor Quarry.

7 Care should be taken in exploring the old quarry workings but visitors are rewarded with an enchanting place full of echoes of the past.

8 Walk along the track north now and on the right you will see another 17th century granite marker like the one you saw back at the antiquities, and off to the left Yellowmead Farm.

9 You will soon reach the main road and on the opposite side a pump house and the ruins of what was the Foggintor Mission Hall with a small caretaker's cottage on one side. Like the children of times past you must walk back down to where the old school once stood, now the car park. Just down the road from here there is the Dartmoor Inn at the bottom of the River Walkham valley.

In August 1896 the Mission Hall was opened as a school for 41 children of the quarry workers. In 1898 there were 60 children and by 1903, 95 pupils from throughout the area crowded into the little building. It was finally closed in 1912 and the children then had to walk down the hill to the new school at 'Four Winds' where your walk started.

The Royal Oak at Meavy.

8 Down Tor

Old farmsteads at Combeshead, Cuckoo Rock, explore a Potato Cave, and a fine stone row.

The car park is a popular place as it is not far from Plymouth. There is a pleasant pub at Meavy, the Royal Oak, and another at Dousland.

Level: 
Length: 4 miles
Terrain: Tracks, and open moorland.
Park & start ref: SX568693
Refreshments: The Royal Oak at Meavy, The Burrator Inn, Dousland.

Cuckoo Rock from the ruins of Combeshead Farm.

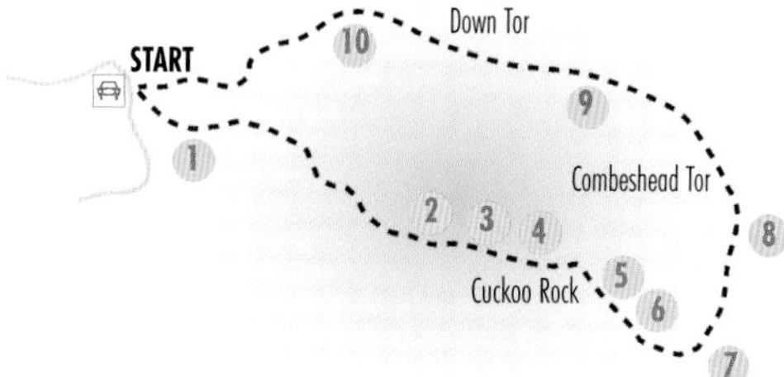

1 Where the road round Burrator Reservoir begins to swing south there is an obvious track that runs along the edge of the forestry plantation in a south-easterly direction. It is easy walking with pleasant glimpses into the forest of mature conifers and some gnarled beeches growing on the mossy banks to your left. You will soon pass a ruined mine building or possibly a barn of the old Middleworth Farm on your right.

2 The rocky lane will lead you towards the ruins of Deancombe Farm. Just before the farm a 'stroll' comes down from Down Tor and this could be one way for you to return.

Stroll is the name given to funnel-shaped walls that lead down from open moorland. These were used when collecting and driving animals down to the lower fields. With ponies this herding is known as the 'pony drift'.

3 Walk on now towards the ruins with a wall on your left with a series of granite blocks or straddles on top, in what was the farm court. All around in the ruins there are massive granite blocks, posts and lintels. A sad sight and a reminder of how well built these old moorland farms were.

Ruins of Deancombe Farm.

Cuckoo Rock.

4 Go on through the farmyard and you will see Cuckoo Rock standing up ahead of you. Walk through the fields and out on to the open moor. Hop across a stream and follow the path that climbs steeply up to the rock.

5 From Cuckoo Rock aim diagonally south-east down across the hill on a rather indistinct path but if you cant find it then aim at the clump of trees in the valley ahead of you; rather rough going. This will bring you down to the ruins of Combeshead Farm.

6 Walk through the old farm gates and after a short distance look for a path that runs uphill left for about 200 yards past some

low walls on the bracken covered slope. After a while in a low, walled bank you will see the entrance to the Potato Cave.

If you wanted to look for another little man-made cave then go back down to the track which you came up to get to the Potato Cave, then turn left and cross the river by jumping it or by the footbridge. Follow the little path uphill and look for a gully which you follow for a short while until you see a low entrance in the hillside.

8 No path to follow now but some route finding to do as you need to work your way north by the stream and in the gully by the tin workings, leaving Combeshead Tor on

It is quite dry and snug inside the Potato Cave. This is where the farmer from Combeshead, old William Pengelly who died in 1932, kept his crop of potatoes dry and at an even temperature. It might also have been used by the local miners too and there is a suggestion that an illicit still was hidden here, with storage for contraband or bootleg liquor.

The Potato Cave.

your left (you could climb it if you wished to bag another summit!). Then aim at the fine stone row about half a mile away.

It is a gentle walk in a westerly direction across to Down Tor, your objective

10 A decision now about routes for the return. (a) You could just take the well-worn path south-west down through the fields of the old farms of Deancombe and Narrator back to the car park. (b) Alternatively you might like to drop down south from Down Tor past a small cairn and some hut circles to find the funnel-shaped walls of the stroll I mentioned earlier. Once you reach the track you turn right and go back the way you came.

Down Tor Stone Row.

Down Tor is one of Dartmoor's finest stone rows with a stone circle at its west end. It has been suggested that the shadows at sunrise of the largest stones predicted the summer solstice. The whole site was ransacked in 1880 and stones taken and knocked over. It was restored in 1884 and it needed 24 workers and a hoist to get the largest stone which weighed 5 tons upright.

Gutter Tor.

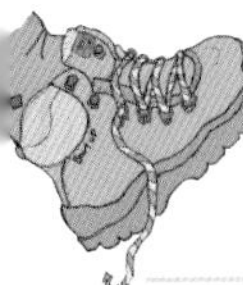

9 Gutter Tor

An old Warren House, the largest menhirs on Dartmoor and a fine stone row.

There is room to park the car at Burcombe Ford on Sheepstor Brook. There is a pleasant pub at Meavy, The Royal Oak.

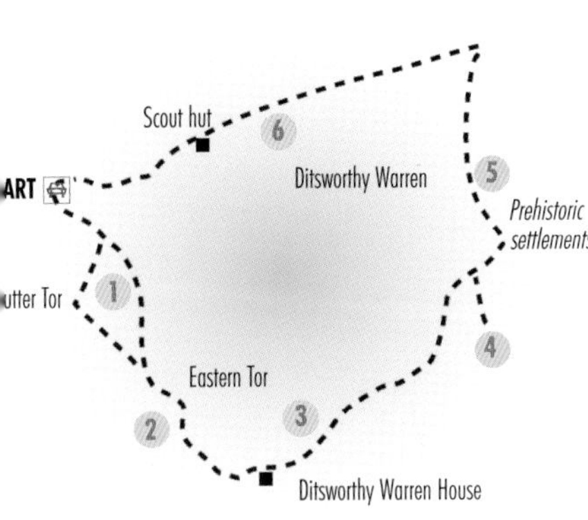

Level:
Length: 3 miles
Terrain: Tracks and open Moorland.
Park & Start ref: SX579673.
Refreshments: The Royal Oak at Meavy

Prehistoric menhir (left) and stone row (below), Drizzlecombe.

(1) Set off along the obvious track south-east below Gutter Tor. Once again you can if you wish leave out the climb to the summit but if you want to get to the top follow the path by the fence to the top.

The name Gutter is unusual. It could be linked to the fact that goats once grazed here. But there are several other possibilities one being that gutter is a leat used by the miners or even that it is a corruption of Cut Tor.

(2) I shall assume you made the summit and that you must make your way back down a grassy path to the track from your peak. They are difficult to find, but there is a vermin trap and the remains of an old longhouse near the track. As the moor opens up into a grassy area you will pass several mounds that are the artificial burrows of Ditsworthy Warren house that you will soon reach.

'Pillow Mounds', artificial rabbit warrens.

(3) Take the track that runs behind Ditsworthy Warren towards the north-east. As it peters out there are a few marshy areas to navigate but it is probably better to keep to the right. You will soon come to an area known as Drizzlecombe

Ditsworthy is one of the many Warren Houses on Dartmoor where rabbits were bred commercially in artificial burrows. Behind the house you will see the kennel court, with stone kennels set into the walls, where the warrener kept his dogs that were used to drive the rabbits into the nets. This Warren House was used until the 1950s.

and its imposing stone row.

I still get a strange prickling sensation in the back of my neck when I am alone in one of the areas of stone rows and hut circles. Almost I can sense and feel the spirits of the Bronze Age people of over 4000 years ago. It is no wonder that Dartmoor has such a huge number of legends and myths.

4 It is worth wandering over to Giant's Basin, a cairn that lies south-east of the rows. I am sure you will want to spend a lot of time looking and wandering through the whole of this fascinating area.

Ditsworthy Warren house.

I know I said that the stone row at Down Tor was one of the best but Drizzlecombe is probably the best! The whole area is the most extraordinary complex of Bronze Age stone circles, long rows, the tallest standing stones on Dartmoor, kists, cairns, hut circles and pounds found in Western Europe. Some of the menhirs were put up after they had fallen, by the great Dartmoor antiquarian R. Hansford Worth in 1893. He found that the largest was 17 feet 10 ins tall and probably weighed 7 tons.

5 When you can tear yourself away then cut up the lovely shallow valley of the stream of Drizzlecombe towards the north-north-east. You will pass another kistvaen (grave) and just before you meet the track that runs down from Eylesbarrow Mine you will see some ruins that were all part of the mining activities here. If you want to find out more about Eylesbarrow Mine then there are details to be found in my book *Dartmoor: Walks into History* published by Halsgrove as are fuller details about some of the walks in this little booklet. You could even walk up to the mine.

6 Turn left and it is an easy walk down the track to the Scout Hut and your car.

Kennels at Ditsworthy.

Drizzlecombe Menhir.

Vixen Tor.

10 Pew Tor

A Dartmoor leat, a windy cross, and a bullseye.

There are places to park off the road on the verges just before Merrivale Quarries, or in the quarry back west along the road . The Dartmoor Inn is just down the road.

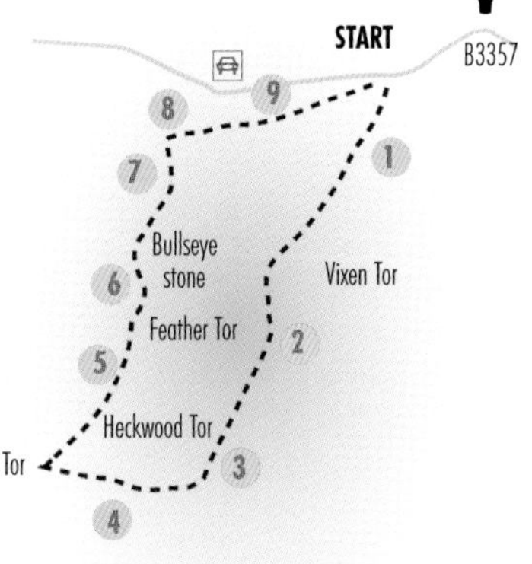

Rowan berries.

Level: 
Length: 3.75 miles
Terrain: Quite a lot of rough moorland walking.
Park & start ref: SX545751.
Public transport: There are buses across the moor in summer.
Refreshments: The Dartmoor Inn at Merrivale.

Dartmoor ponies.

1 The first part of this walk follows the footpaths that are shown on the 1:25,000 maps. Set off south-west along the wall aiming towards Vixen Tor. From a certain viewpoint the tor is said to resemble an old man wearing a cap, standing with his back to his wife! Or from further west it resembles the Egyptian Sphinx. By the wall there is the boundary stone for the Whitchurch-Sampford parishes.

2 Swing south now down to the stream which you cross at the ford by stepping stones. This can be a problem after heavy rain. Start the climb up the hill and pass by another boundary stone. Start the climb up the hill and pass by another boundary stone which marks the meeting of Sampford Spiney and Whitchurch parishes.

Walkers and climbers are not allowed to walk across to the tor inside the walled area. This is not the place to raise controversial issues but for many years access was possible. Indeed I have climbed here with Chris Bonington. Legend has it that there was a witch of Vixen Tor who lured travellers across the moor into the sucking, deep mires nearby. So watch out!

3 It is worth climbing up Heckwood Tor to get the fine views down the lovely, wooded valley of the River Walkham below you to the east.

4 Work your way across to Pew Tor. You might find the path but otherwise aim across the open moorland. You will cross the leat that comes all the way from near Feather Tor and Windypost Cross where you will be going next.

Pew Tor is shaped almost like a castle with a central grassy courtyard with four granite towers in each corner. The views from here are tremendous, standing as it does on the edge of Dartmoor. You can see down to Mount Edgcumbe on the other side of Plymouth, the Channel and to where the Tavy joins the Tamar just above Saltash.

5 Your route now lies more or less north as you aim at the low lying rocks of Feather Tor by following the obvious track.

The 6 foot cross at Windy Post has an apt name as it is indeed a bleak windswept site. Both the Abbots' Way and the Jobbers' Path came this way. The name Jobber or Joblers comes from the woollen industry, as this was the name given to the man who bought and sold wool. In the leat near the cross you will see a typical, traditional Dartmoor invention. It is a sluice gate called a bull's-eye stone. You will see the stone with a hole cut in the middle to control the flow of water.

Windy Post Cross.

Unfinished wheelwrights's stone.

Right: The bull's-eye stone.

6 From the top of Feather Tor you will see Windy Post Cross ahead of you so walk down the gentle slope towards it and the leat.

7 Follow the bank of the leat more or less north. You will pass a little ruin that was called The Blacksmith's Shop which perhaps was once connected to mining in the area. Nearby you will also see another abandoned, dressed and carved piece of granite said to be an unfinished wheelwright's stone.

8 Cross over the little granite clapper bridge on your right and aim back south and down to the pretty little ford. However it might interest you keep along north to have a look at the aqueduct where the Grimstone and Sortridge Leat crosses the stream and then come back to the clapper bridge.

9 All that is left now is to follow the tracks back east to the car.

Vixen Tor with King Tor beyond.

Epilogue

My dear friend Eric Shipton, probably the greatest mountaineer and explorer of all time, wrote in his marvellous autobiography;

" The springs of enchantment lie within ourselves; they arise from our sense of wonder, that most precious of gifts, the birthright of every child. Lose it and life becomes flat and colourless; keep it and 'All experience is an arch wherethro' Gleams that untravell'd World, whose margin fades For ever and for ever when I move.'"

I hope that through this little book, as you climbed your tors, you may have found your own "springs of enchantment" and this "sense of wonder". You will have seen the huge skies and felt, I am sure, the profound feeling of loneliness of the wild, primeval moor with its secret corners, deep valleys and tumbling streams. On some days, maybe when perhaps you shouldn't have come out, you will have had to lean into the fierce winds with mist and rain sweeping across the landscape in fury, resenting your intrusion. On other days all will be quiet and still in the hot, summer sun with only the skylarks' bubbling trills to cut across the heavy silence.

I am sure you will have felt the magic and mystery of this hauntingly beautiful wilderness and if you didn't climb all the tors this time I hope you will come back again and again to a truly hypnotic Dartmoor.

The author at Drizzlecombe.